"A... ... and challenges that she faced from childhood on. It is a reminder…that 'all things work together for the good of those who love the Lord and are called according to His purpose.'"

Dale Poseley, Bible Teacher
Crackpots Ministry

"Dolores Bennett knows how to tell a story! Through an almost Huckleberry Finn upbringing in a poor Filipino family, Dolores weaves a redemptive story through her own fears and failures that bring hope and encouragement to everyone. I highly recommend His Hand on Me to anyone who enjoys high, real-life adventure… with profound, life-altering truths in every chapter."

Brenda Murphy PhD
President & CEO, SailAway

His
Hand
on
Me

His Hand on Me

Dolores D. Bennett

edited by Kara Schiller

XULON PRESS

Xulon Press
2301 Lucien Way #415
Maitland, FL 32751
407.339.4217
www.xulonpress.com

© 2020 by Dolores D. Bennett

All rights reserved solely by the author. The author guarantees all contents are original and do not infringe upon the legal rights of any other person or work. No part of this book may be reproduced in any form without the permission of the author. The views expressed in this book are not necessarily those of the publisher.

Unless otherwise indicated, Scripture quotations taken from the New King James Version (NKJV). Copyright © 1982 by Thomas Nelson, Inc. Used by permission. All rights reserved.

Printed in the United States of America.

Paperback ISBN-13: 978-1-63221-778-3
eBook ISBN-13: 978-1-6322-1779-0

Table of Contents

Introduction xiii

Chapter 1: Duck Eggs and Pancakes 1

Chapter 2: The Rolling Drum 5

Chapter 3: My Grand Escapade
and Fearing for My Head 11

Chapter 4: "Work" in Sagada. 19

Chapter 5: Stealing White Rabbit
and Being Forgiven 23

Chapter 6: My Name Is Pain 29

Chapter 7: Being Super Scared 35

Chapter 8: Searching for Something
and Wishing My
Father Loved Me 39

Chapter 9: Need for Beauty and Grace 49

Chapter 10:	Silent Fight with Father and My Regret	55
Chapter 11:	Chased by Fear but Finding Faith in Jesus	63
Chapter 12:	Winding Toy and Reconquering Fear	69
Chapter 13:	Faith that Moves Mountains and Gets Jobs	75
Chapter 14:	Meeting Joe	83
Chapter 15:	Being a Professional Driver in the US	87
Chapter 16:	Going Back to the Thing About My Name	93
Chapter 17:	The Desire to Learn Spanish and Go to the Mission Field by Faith	99
Chapter 18:	"Your work place is your mission field."	105
Chapter 19:	Being Thankful in Times of Trouble	111
Chapter 20:	Making Money but Losing Time	121
Chapter 21:	Discovering My Platform	125

Dedication

I would like to dedicate this book to my siblings: James, Marie, Carol, Walter, Annie and to my late sister Emily, as well as to my late parents Pablo and Elena Domanog, who helped me become what I am today.

Acknowledgments

I would like to give my endless thanks to my cousin Jane Doyayag Capacio for being with me from the conception of this book to its completion, and for doing anything I asked her to do to help me out. I would also like to thank the three people who made a writer out me by encouraging me to write my story: Ruth P. Tingda, Dr. Brenda Murphy and Ms. Louise Jenkins. Last but not least, I would like to thank my editor Kara Schiller for doing more than an editor's job. Without any of you, I couldn't have finished this book. May God bless you all!

Introduction

When the Taal Volcano erupted in the Philippines on January 12, 2020, Dolores Bennett packed her bags to go help the victims because she had five friends living near the volcano. After doing relief work and Bible studies in the city of Batangas, Dolores went on to Sagada, and then to Baguio City to visit her family and some former high school classmates. It was her last day in Baguio City when she finally had the chance to call Ruth, her childhood friend and neighbor, to fulfill a long-awaited promise to have dinner with Ruth's mother, Aunt Julia.

Two years prior to this meeting, Dolores had been visiting Baguio City when she and Ruth met unexpectedly over a cup of coffee.

When Ruth went home and told her mother about their talk, Aunt Julia got excited – she wanted to meet with Dolores too; she had been wondering what had happened to her. Unfortunately, Dolores had already left Baguio city. She promised Aunt Julia, through Ruth, that she would meet with her when she returned. Finally, the day had arrived for the meeting.

Dolores was the last one to arrive at the restaurant. Aunt Julia and Ruth, plus Ruth's friend Louisa, were already waiting. Aunt Julia came prepared with all the questions she'd been wanting to ask her. As soon as the author sat down and started digging into the food, Aunt Julia started asking questions. The story began. One by one the scenes came alive in Dolores's mind as she responded to Aunt Julia's questions.

Are you are wondering how Aunt Julia became the author's aunt even though they are not biologically related? It is because Aunt Julia was a close friend of Dolores' late mother Elena. Yet even if she were not, Dolores would still have called her "aunt" because in the

Philippines, older adults are referred to as "aunts" and "uncles" as a means of respect.

All the names mentioned in the story are true. They are real people, and yes, all of them are all still alive. In fact, they are all still living in the Mountain Province of the Philippines, specifically in Baguio City, which is the summer capital of the country.

Mankayan and Sagada are the two places where most of this story unfolded when the author was young. The distance between the two towns is just a little more than two hours. It took more than a day for the author to travel that distance when she ran away as a child because she was taking bus hikes. Moreover, there was a typhoon that day that caused landslides which forced them to go down from the bus and do some walking in between bus riding. Bontoc and Besao are neiboring towns of Sagada.

Mankayan was known for its mines; specifically, the Lepanto Mining Company. This company brought various people from different provinces, including the author's parents, to Mankayan. Sagada is no longer the quiet town the author knew when she was young. Back then, each family raised their own food. Today, most people's livelihood depends heavily on tourism. Sagada is a popular tourist spot because of its rice terraces, caves, and hanging coffins.

Dolores has family members and relatives still living in Sagada, so she still visits the place every time she goes to the Philippines.

Chapter 1

Duck Eggs and Pancakes

"Where were your parents?" Aunt Julia asked her third question before I'd even had a chance to shovel a delectable piece of tortilla, fresh from the frying pan, into my mouth.

"I do not know," I confessed. "All I can remember is that there were my two younger siblings and me, and that I provided our food by stealing it."

"Stealing?" Aunt Julia, Ruth, and Louisa gasped in unison. Their disapproving eyes demanded an explanation.

Smiling, and as animated as I could be, I began to tell the childhood story I'd never shared before. I finally felt confident enough to tell the truth because I was no longer the person I used to be. How did that happen? Well, 2 Corinthians 5:17 says, 'Therefore, if anyone is in Christ, he is a new creation; old things have passed away; behold, all things have become new.' That's me now; a new creation.

"We were hungry," I explained, "so I stole our neighbors' duck eggs and cooked them, and then we ate them before the Tugad's came to investigate. They knew the culprit had come from our house because of the footprints that I'd left. But they could not prove they were my footprints because they were bigger than my feet. The rain saved me that day; it made the soil slippery, so I slid unintentionally and it made my footprints bigger than they were."

They all burst into laughter, which filled The House of Yolo Yoghurt in Baguio and made us aware that we weren't the only customers.

Encouraged by their response, I admitted to another escapade: "I stole pancakes, too," I blurted out. Again, they laughed. They were all ears, so I continued.

"It was from the same neighbor. I stole some of the leftover pancakes they'd been bragging about that day when they knew we had nothing to eat. I climbed through an opening in their kitchen when they all went to bed. I believe their radio helped me out that night; their ears were glued to it and they couldn't hear the creaking sound of plates being flipped over."

Again, we all broke into laughter. Then came an unexpected remark from Louisa: "What a survival skill you had!" They all nodded in agreement.

I was relieved that they considered my thievery a survival skill and not something worse. It came as such a surprise that they were really entertained by my story; I hadn't expected that.

"How old were you at the time?" asked Aunt Julia.

Before I could respond, Ruth interrupted to prepare me for the barrage of questions to come. "My mother has been asking me so many questions about you that I could not answer, so I told her to ask you all her questions herself."

I looked at Auntie Julia and answered, "I was not going to school yet, so I believe I was about six years old."

Aunt Julia sighed. "I wish the Tugads were still alive so you could go tell them your stories and bless them."

"Me too!" I agreed. Suddenly, a light bulb went on in my head; *What a brilliant idea!* I thought, and then said aloud, "I can certainly tell these stories to their children one day."

I shared a prayer of gratitude with them to the One who had lavishly blessed me: 'Thank you God that I do not have to steal food any more in order to survive! And we all expressed a heartfelt "Amen!"

Chapter 2

THE ROLLING DRUM

"WAIT!" RUTH INTERRUPTED AS I began to answer another question. "Let's order your food first before you continue because we already ordered ours." Aunt Julia, Ruth, and Louisa had arrived a few minutes before me because I'd forgotten that I had a dentist appointment before our dinner that evening. I was so hungry when I arrived that all I'd said was, "Hello everyone!" and immediately reached for those irresistible tortillas.

After placing my order, I asked. "Where was I?"

"You were about to say something about your older siblings," said Ruth.

"Oh yes!" I responded. Then I continued.

"My older siblings had returned home. I found out from them that our mother was doing some farm work and that my father was in Abra, another province. With my older siblings back, I was suddenly demoted; I was no longer the oldest in the house.

"I thought life would be better for me when my older siblings arrived, but it went from bad to worse. I must have been a terribly naughty girl because I was always getting into trouble. My older brothers and sisters had to discipline their 'pain of a sister,' but I was sneaky.

"To avoid punishment, I often ran away. I would leave the house before they came home in the evenings and then sneak back home to eat in the morning after they'd all left for work or school. I slept anywhere I could rest my little head.

"Often, this meant sleeping at a friend's house. I alternated which friends I stayed with so I wouldn't be such a burden on families who had little more than we did. I didn't want my friends being scolded for bringing home another mouth to feed. Sometimes I slept in the corridor of a boarding house up the hill from our house.

"When I ran out of options, I slept under our house where the firewood was piled. That was the most undesirable place for me to sleep, though, because my siblings could discover my hideout if they came down to get firewood. The only benefit to that spot was that I could hear what was going on in the house and anything they might be saying about me. It made me feel like I was outsmarting them," I grinned.

Louisa giggled and I continued, "One evening, the urge to run away was so strong. Not caring what the weather would be like, what kind of trouble I'd be in, or what kind of punishment I'd receive, I left home in the afternoon for the umpteenth time before anyone arrived.

"That night was different from all the previous nights, though; it stormed! It was raining so hard that all my friends' doors were already shut tight and I was too ashamed to knock. The boarding house's corridor was wet. My only option was to sleep beneath our house, so I nestled between piles of wood. It was terribly uncomfortable; the wind was so strong it cut to my skin. *I need a different place to sleep,* I thought.

"I looked out into the yard and noticed that the drum that we used to ripen bananas was lying in our yard. I crawled in and sat in the middle to try to keep the drum balanced. It was a tight fit but it must have been comfortable enough because the storm lulled me to sleep.

"In the middle of the night I was awakened suddenly when I found myself tumbling around inside the drum![1] I had fallen asleep and tipped over, which started the drum rolling! The strong wind pushed the drum down the hill toward the canal. Panicked, I thought I was going to die, when it suddenly stopped.

---

[1] While I was writing this particular part of the story, I was also doing a Bible study in the book of Judges. I came across the story of a man telling his dream to his companion; about "a loaf of barley bread that tumbled into the camp of Midian; it came to a tent and struck it, so that it fell and overturned, and the tent collapsed" (Judges 7:13), which made me laugh.

"I don't know what stopped the drum, but I was thankful to not be flipping over anymore. I was too dizzy to think or move, so I stayed inside the drum until the storm had passed. When I finally crawled out, I saw that banana trees had caught the drum before it reached the canal that was overflowing with raging water. I could have been swallowed up! Whew!" I sighed.

They roared with laughter. I looked around to see if we were disturbing other customers, but the only other people in the restaurant were two young men at another table who didn't seem bothered.

When they calmed down a bit, I said, "It must not have been my time to die, because it was not luck that saved me; it was the hand of the Lord. Looking back, I believe He sent his angels to protect me that night. Psalms 91:11 says, 'For He will give his angels charge over you, to keep you in all your ways.'"

They nodded, reflectively. I took a sip of my tea and began the next story.

Chapter 3

My Grand Escapade and Fearing for My Head

"After that, I saw no relief on the horizon for me, so I decided to run as far away as I could and never come back. My young mind was racing, *But where? Ah! I know – I should go to Sagada!*

"When I decided to go live with my grandparents, I went to sleep early that night and woke up early the next day. A trip to Sagada at that time required a day of travel by bus. The following morning, as soon as my older siblings were gone, I ran to the market to catch the first bus out of town before anyone noticed I was gone.

"As soon as I got on the bus, the driver asked, 'Who are you traveling with?' I had practiced my answer beforehand, so I said with confidence, "My mother will be following me as soon as she is done washing clothes.

"I must have been convincing because he let me on the bus without questioning me further. I was so young I didn't even have to pay for a ticket. I'd already factored that into my decision to go to Sagada; you see, once, my grandfather visited us and brought me by bus to Sagada and I learned that children were not charged fare. I was glad I did not have to pay because all I had with me was my bag of toys," I chuckled.

"Bag of toys!" Louisa laughed. She and Ruth chuckled together.

"After 30 minutes, we reached the stop at Abatan. From there, I had to catch another bus to get to Sagada. As soon as I got off the bus, I saw a friendly old lady who looked like my grandmother's sister, so I befriended her and told her I was traveling alone to Sagada.

"She said she was going to Bontoc, a town an hour away from Sagada. I must have looked so innocent and pitiful to her; she immediately took me under wing. She fed me and took care of me. Perhaps she, too, was an angel sent by God to look after me.

"What this nice lady did not know was that I was thinking terrible thoughts about her in my little head. I had developed a fear of the people from Bontoc. I'd heard horror stories from my older family members, who'd been tasked with putting us kids to sleep, about how they were head hunters, and how they'd sacrifice people's heads to their 'anitos;' their gods. Honestly, I was horrified that she might be luring me to her hometown to cut off my head! I didn't have any choice, however, but to go along with her and just stay on the alert.

"I prepared a plan of escape ahead of time; when we reached Bontoc I would sleep in her house, but before she woke up in the morning to cut off my head, I would be gone. I would run to the bus station and finish my trip to Sagada."

I paused when the waitress stopped at our table. "Need some more tea or water?" she asked.

"Tea, please!" I quickly answered. I handed her my empty glass and then resumed my story.

"Fortunately for me, I did not have to execute my brilliant plan because before we reached Bontoc, a couple got onto our bus who were going to Besao, a town beyond Sagada. When the nice old lady found out, she implored them to take me along and drop me off in Sagada.

"What a relief! I felt guilty about my suspicious thoughts towards her, but I didn't have time to entertain my guilt because I had to come up with a quick plan to protect myself from this new couple.

"The couple had a private vehicle waiting for them at the crossroads that leads to Bontoc and Sagada. Again, my suspicious tendency kicked in. Or perhaps God gave me discretion that will protect me like it says in Proverbs 2:11.

"All I knew was that I shouldn't trust anyone, regardless of their kindness toward me. I was not sure if this couple would really drop me off in Sagada. What if they kidnapped me and forced me to be their maid? There were so many things they could do to take advantage of my situation."

Suddenly, like an unexpected storm, a wave of cheerful noise flooded the restaurant. It was a group of college students in their white uniforms. The atmosphere changed from cozy to noisy. We watched, as each student ran hastily to a table to secure a seat. We were still watching them when Aunt Julia brought us back to the story. "I can't believe you were thinking of all those things at such a young age!"

I nodded my head in agreement and then proceeded, "As soon as we reached Sagada and the vehicle slowed down, I jumped out without saying a word. I ran like a wild animal that had been set free. I didn't slow down until I reached my grandparents' house. By then, it was 9:00 pm and dark. Since I was exhausted and afraid, and had no explanation for why I was there, I sat in utter silence and ignored all my grandparents' questions. I didn't speak one word until the next morning. I was just glad I'd arrived safely.

"Back at home, they were searching for me. After a week with no luck, my eldest brother, James, decided to go to Sagada to tell my grandparents that I'd disappeared. Remember this was before cell phones and email. The only way they could communicate was through telegrams, but even that had been cut off because of a storm.

"There was a landslide so bus travel was slow and James and a friend traveled by foot most of the way. They arrived around 8:00 pm on the first night of a town fiesta. I was at the municipal hall watching the show when, much to my surprise, the loud speaker announced, 'Our next number is a song from James Doyayag.' I was shocked! He must have gotten off the bus and been pulled in by someone to perform a song. Back then, he was quite a popular singer.

"I started trembling and couldn't even appreciate his song because all I could think of was how to avoid his wrath. I imagined all the things that he might do to me for having run away for so long. I had to come up with a plan quickly. As soon as he got down from the stage, I went to him with tears streaming down my face, hoping it would soften his heart.

"My tactic worked! James did not get angry at all! He was overjoyed to see me. He hugged me and cried. I cried with him, but this time my crying was real. I did not realize his love and concern for me until that night. He left early the following day to tell my family that I was alive. That was all that had mattered to him."

"I don't remember your brother James at all," reflected Ruth.

"Maybe because back then, we didn't know each other yet," I explained and then began to tell them about my life in Sagada.

Chapter 4

"Work" in Sagada

"Life with my grandparents meant plenty of food and no older siblings to worry about whenever I got into trouble. But I had to work, work, work. The word 'play' was not in my grandparents' vocabulary. As soon as they woke up, they went to the fields to work and so did I.

"I was glad when school opened and my grandfather enrolled me in first grade. School gave me the perfect escape from working in the fields. It was an opportunity to do school work, which I loved, and it was also a place for me to play.

"My grandparent made sure I got home right after school to do chores. Sometimes I defiantly left whatever chore I was doing and went to play, knowing full well that when I came back, I would be chewed out. I believe that the adage, 'sticks and stones may break my bones, but words will never hurt me' described me well. I was willing to endure words, loud words, even threatening words if it meant I'd get a chance to play.

"One thing I can say about my grandparents is that they never spanked me… no, I take that back. My grandfather whipped me just once. But I very much deserved it.

"It was late in the afternoon, and it was time to cook supper. My cousin Ngali and I were having the time of our lives weaving belts out of dried banana bark. Then came the voice of the party pooper: 'Dolor! Ngali! It is time to cook!' That was my grandfather calling us to stop whatever we were doing and come do our chores

"As you know, our culture and upbringing demanded that we obey immediately when called to do something, whether we wanted to or not. But this time, instead of doing what my grandfather wanted me to do, I let my anger get a hold of me. I picked up a bamboo broom and whipped my grandfather's leg, which had already been hurting because of a previous fall.

"Before I could run away, he grabbed me, pinned me down and whipped me. I knew it was my fault, but that did not stop me from crying loudly like I was going to die. Not knowing what to do next, I did what I did best back then: I ran away. I wish someone had taught me that 'Fools give full vent to their rage' like it says in Proverbs 29:11. Perhaps it would've helped me stop acting like a fool.

"That night, my grandmother could not find Ngali or me since Ngali had decided to run away too. She asked Ngali's father to help her search our friends' houses. He found us and he, too, gave way to his anger. He was about to pound us with a piece of wood as big as a baseball bat but our grandmother was right behind him and she grabbed the wood out of his hands before it hit us. She screamed at the top of her lungs, 'I asked you to help me find them, not kill them!' Like me, Ngali's father also allowed his anger to make him act like a fool."

"Wow! What an experience for a little girl." commented Louisa as she reached for her drink.

"But I had a lot more," I replied with a smile. As soon as she put her drink down, she gestured for me to go on.

Chapter 5

STEALING WHITE RABBIT AND BEING FORGIVEN

"After I finished first grade, my older sister Emily came to take me back to Mankayan where we lived. My grandmother did not want me to go with my sister but Emily would not go back to Mankayan without me, so I went back with her.

"Back home with my siblings again, things were a little better. We were still poor but at least we were eating. Second grade, however, turned out to be the most embarrassing year of my life because my stealing finally caught up with me. I got caught stealing and eating White Rabbit candies and I was branded with the disgraceful name: 'Mangakew si White Rabbit'; the 'one who steals White Rabbit.' My classmate, Harry, gave me the nickname.

"You see, our teacher, Mrs. Aspiras, entrusted me with her basket of White Rabbit candies. She asked me to watch her basket for a few minutes. But those few minutes gave me all the opportunity I needed to pocket enough candies for me and my classmates.

"When Mrs. Aspiras saw those candies being passed around during class she was so furious that she stopped teaching and, with fiery eyes, delivered an angry sermon just for me."

Ruth began laughing, "So that was your third stealing escapade! But this time it sounds like a Robin Hood story; you stole from the rich to give to the poor!" The women were all laughing now.

"Yes!" I agreed, and jokingly added, "I guess you could call me little Ms. Robin Hood."

"Anyway, that was how I got caught. But that time I didn't do it for survival. The temptation to eat those inviting candies was just too strong for me to resist. If I knew then what I know now – that God does not allow us to be tempted beyond our ability to endure, *(1 Corinthians 10:13)* I could have saved myself from Mrs. Aspiras' wrath, and I wouldn't have been given a despicable nickname to endure for the rest of the year.

"In third grade, I was so relieved that Harry was not in my class anymore! Although I still hid from him every time I saw him, it was much easier on me and I was thankful. That year was like a fresh start and I had the chance to come out of my shell and be vibrant and friendly again.

"For the first time, I'd met a friend who accepted me for who I was. Through our friendship, I discovered another ugly thing about myself: envy. I did not realize how much I envied her until I hurt her. I compared myself to her and found her better than I was. No wonder Paul instructed the Corinthians not to compare themselves to one another; 'But they, measuring themselves by themselves, and comparing themselves among themselves, are not wise' *(2 Corinthians 10:12).*

"I believe Rosemarie was a God-sent friend to teach me lessons. Not through her words, necessarily, but through her actions. From the beginning, she was so generous to me; she brought a box of candies to sell at school and every time she ate one, she gave me one to eat as well.

"Then I got sneaky. Instead of eating what she shared, I started saving the candies until I had a box of my own. Then I sold them when she wasn't around."

Ruth and Louisa started giggling again. They were both amused by my undercover business.

"Rosemarie was also very forgiving," I continued. "At the end of the year, when our teacher called both of us to the front of the class and announced that Rosemarie had earned top honors and I was in second, I envied her. At the height of my envy, I pushed her down the stairs. She had bruises on her legs! When she started crying, I realized I was in big trouble, and I didn't know what to do to make things right.

"I felt so bad but I couldn't even bring myself to say 'I'm sorry.'

Suddenly, she stood up and asked, 'Where are we going to play?' At that moment, I realized she'd forgiven me. Perhaps the joy she felt at being first in our class made her forget the pain I'd inflicted on her. She was someone that Proverbs 17:17 perfectly describes: 'A friend loves at all times.'"

I paused for a moment and sipped on my drink while we reflected on that truth from God's word. I was indeed fortunate to have a friend who loved me in spite of myself.

Chapter 6

MY NAME IS PAIN

"My experience in third grade didn't cure me; I continued to be a troublemaker. My fourth grade teacher threw an eraser at me to get my attention!" I smiled. The women snickered and shook their heads.

"Thankfully, she missed. But then she screamed at me for interrupting her train of thought. When my classmates saw that it was me who always caused our teacher to get angry, they ganged up on me. I couldn't see everyone's eyes but I felt them all glaring at me as our teacher delivered her final threat: 'I will drop you from the honor roll!'

"I was so embarrassed. It made me wonder why was I so different from the rest. Why was I the only one behaving like a monster and causing such distraction in the classroom.[2] I bowed my head in shame, resigned to receive my consequence. I knew I was in deep trouble and no amount of apologizing would get me out of it because this was not my first offense. I wished I knew how to make things right and to save myself from punishment. I was even more concerned with being punished at home when my parents found out that I'd gotten in trouble in school again.

"Scared that I would make matters worse, I succumbed to silence until the last day of school. Surprisingly, my teacher never told

---

[2] When I became an elementary school teacher in Tennessee, I learned that there were students like me who could not keep themselves from getting into trouble. I was told that they had ADHD and had to be medicated. That was when it dawned on me that I must have had ADHD when I was younger. Since few knew about ADHD in the Philippines back then, I was spared from the medication. Honestly, I don't know which one would have been worse: medication or punishment?

on me. I don't know what made her change her mind but I'm glad she did."

I paused for a moment before continuing because I knew what I said next would come as a shock. "I must not have learned my lesson, though, because in fifth grade, my history teacher threw her high heeled shoe at me!"

My friends' eyebrows all shot up. "What on earth did you do?" asked Aunt Julia.

"I can't remember what I did. But I do remember that the next year, in sixth grade, my home economics teacher, Mrs. Garcia, whipped me with a stick because she caught me playing outside when my classmates were already in the classroom working.

"This was around the time when I learned that my first name, Dolores, means 'pain' or 'sorrow' in Spanish. I'm sure my parents didn't know that when they chose my name. They would never have cursed me unintentionally or cursed themselves with a 'pain-inducing' daughter. To everyone, I was such a rascal.

"That's why I never I understood why Mrs. Garcia invited me to go live with her family in their humongous house right after she whipped me. Of course I gladly accepted her invitation. Who wouldn't?"

They nodded and I continued, "To me, a big house meant lots of food and plenty of good things I didn't have, and I was right! I was well fed and Mrs. Garcia taught me how to bake, clean the house thoroughly, and other things I'd never learned before because I'd always been running.

"When her daughter, Janet, who was about my age, realized how good it was to have someone to play and do chores with, she did not want me to go home. I stayed with them until the end of the school year. Living with them kept me from getting into trouble because if we weren't playing, we were working. I guess Mrs. Garcia knew what she was doing."

"Right after sixth grade, Janet went to Canada so I decided to leave too, despite Mrs. Garcia's offer for me to stay until I finished high school. She even offered to send me to college afterwards. But as a sixth grader, secondary school and college didn't appeal to me. I just wanted to have fun. I decided I'd go back to Sagada where Ngali and my other cousins lived."

Chapter 7

BEING SUPER SCARED

"Seventh grade was a year of ghosts and spirits that haunted me at night." I continued. Aunt Julia nodded, knowingly.

"My enemies came alive at night. Shadows looked like phantoms which were following or watching me. They never touched me, but I felt their presence and they scared me so badly I couldn't sleep at night. I felt they had the upper hand because they were invisible and made me fearful, which rendered me defeated and useless. I decided to leave Sagada for good.

"It wasn't until adulthood that I found out who my enemies were through Paul's vivid description in Ephesians six: 'For we wrestle against flesh and blood, but against principalities, against powers, against the rules of the darkness of this age, against spiritual hosts of wickedness in the heavenly places.'

"It all began when my grandfather got sick. My grandmother and I would go to a mountain that had big rocks piled one on top of the other. She would butcher and cook a chicken there and offer it as a sacrifice to the spirits of the dead. She pleaded with them to help my grandfather get well. That gave me the idea that the spirits of the dead had power to heal the living. Later, I learned that the dead also had the power to hurt the living. This belief did not sit well with me. The more I struggled with this belief the more I feared the dead. They couldn't physically hurt me, but I believed they could, and so I feared them.

"From then on, every time I was told someone had died, I couldn't sleep because I felt that eerie figures lurked around me. When someone in our school died, we were required to attend the service at the chapel. I lay awake all night afterwards. I could see the coffin and hear the songs that we sang clearly as if I were still in the chapel. From then on, I did not want to sleep at my grandparents' house anymore.

"I told my grandparents that I needed my friend to help me with my assignments so that they would let me leave. Then one night, while sleeping at my friend's house, I felt like I was about to vomit, so I stood up and opened the window and vomited. I kept vomiting until I had nothing left to throw up. My stomach began to ache. I ached until I was wrenching in pain. I thought I was about to die, so I called my friend and told her to warn all of my siblings not to ever come to Sagada because the spirits were going to kill them like they were killing me.

"My friend's grandmother sent her to fetch my grandmother in the middle of the night. When my grandmother arrived, she announced, 'Do not ever speak to her again because your breath is rotten.' I suddenly realized that she was talking to my aunt who had died a long time ago. After she uttered those words, my pain immediately subsided. That reinforced my belief that the dead can hurt the living.

"The final straw was when my grandfather died; I just knew I couldn't live there anymore. After his funeral, when the day came for everyone to leave, I stood up first and announced that I was leaving too. They were stunned. They asked me to stay for my grandmother – they begged me to stay! They promised me the moon, they threatened me... but nothing worked. The only thing that moved me was when my grandmother began crying and pleaded, 'Please do not go! Your grandfather left me and now you are going to leave me, too?'

"But her pitiful condition and my love for her did not change my decision because my fear of the dead was greater than my pity for my grandmother. I wanted to justify my decision to leave, but I knew that even if I could articulate how I felt, they wouldn't understand how scared I was. I was determined to leave that day; otherwise, I just knew I would die of fear. Defying them all, I left with the confidence that I was doing the right thing.

Chapter 8

SEARCHING FOR SOMETHING AND WISHING MY FATHER LOVED ME

AUNT JULIA RAISED HER HAND to stop me and said "Before you proceed, let me get this straight. After sixth grade, you went back to Sagada for seventh grade, and then after your grandfather died, you came back to Mankayan again because of your fear of the dead?"

I nodded and explained, "At least in Mankayan, they had different cultural beliefs.

Although there were some who believed in the power of the dead, most of the people did not, or at least they did not practice the rituals. As soon as I arrived in Mankayan, I started my search for something to ease my fears. I really didn't know what I was searching for. I thought I might find it in church, so I attended all of the churches in our town – Catholic, Anglican, Iglesia ni Cristo, UCCP – the United Churches of Christ in the Philippines, Jehovah's Witnesses, and even a church that held their services in the afternoons at the UCCP church.

"While attending these different churches, the church that met every Sunday afternoon at the UCCP church attracted my attention the most. I liked their songs. I found out later that those songs are called hymns. As soon as they started singing, I would sneak in and sing my heart out with them and then sneak back out before dismissal so no-one would notice me. It's not surprising that despite what I was doing, I was still a spiritual wreck.

"At home, I got to live with my mother and father; all of my older siblings were gone.

I was back to being the oldest child again. My mother would leave early in the mornings, before we woke up, to deliver the clothes she had washed and ironed. Then she would come home with pandesal.[3] For us, that was a real treat."

I must have paused to reminisce for a moment, because Aunt Julia interrupted my thoughts when she asked, "What about your father?"

"Well, my father was at home," I responded. I hesitated to continue but I knew I had to, so I proceeded carefully in order to avoid any misinterpretation of what I was about to say.

"Before I say anything about my father," I began, "I would like you to know that I loved him. I'm not sure he ever loved me because he never expressed it... ah, wait! Yes, there was one time that he showed me he cared. He made a Christmas tree out of orange twigs when I went to visit. I was already an adult then." I smiled at the memory, but then grew somber again.

---

[3] Soft Filipino bread rolls.

"I want you to know that I never hated my father. The only reason I did what I did was to teach him a lesson. At least that's what I thought. What I did not take into account was that I did not know the day or hour he was going to die. As Job 14:5 says, 'Since his days are determined, the number of his months is with You; You have appointed his limits that he cannot pass.'

"Only God knew when his appointed time would be and He makes that clear in Hebrews 9:27 when He says 'Inasmuch as it is appointed for men to die once after that comes judgment.' I did not consider that each of us has a death appointment with God and that He alone knows when.

"Unexpectedly, what I did boomeranged. When my father died, I lost the opportunity to make things right. I bemoaned what I did. I cried out, 'I should not have done what I did!' I beat myself up with regrets. If I knew the suffering that guilt would bring him, I would not have done what I did. Proverbs 16:18 phrases it well, 'Pride goes before destruction; a haughty spirit before fall.' That is exactly what my pride brought me: devastation!

"Like Paul, I experienced the inner struggle that made him cry out his frustration; 'For what I am doing, I do not understand. For what I will to do, that I do not practice, but what I hate, that I do *(Romans 7:15)*...'O wretched man that I am! Who will deliver me from this body of death?' *(Romans 7:24)*. But I am glad Paul did not end with that hopeless question! In victory, he concluded, 'I thank God – through Jesus Christ our Lord!' *(Romans 7:25)* I am indeed thankful that I have a God who can work through my messes, and a God who forgives every time I confess *(1 John 1:9)*."

I must have looked pensive because their silence hung in the air for a few seconds until the waiter announced, "Here are more hot tortillas!"

"Yay!" we responded collectively as we happily dug in again, savoring the delightfully fresh tortillas.

Aunt Julia took that opportunity to ask another question, one that required me to go further into the past. "What is it that happened between you and your father?" she asked.

"I remember my father reading all day," I began slowly, "I think he was smart. If he wasn't reading, he was playing cards. When evening came, he would go to the store to drink with his friends and I would lie awake until he came home drunk screaming for light. Then I would get up with my flashlight to light his path and once he was inside, I would prepare his food. While he ate, he would ridicule me, saying, 'You are ugliest among my children and you will never amount to anything.'

"That was our evening routine and that was his daily message to me. I never got mad at him because he never spoke those words when he was sober, so I attributed his mockery to alcohol.

"One day, I needed to practice a declamation piece in front of the mirror. I had just started when I caught my father looking at me with disdain, so I stopped. He blurted out those mocking words again.

"I wasn't sure whether he was drunk or not, but I decided right then that I would prove him wrong. I was in my third year of high school and I had already realized that my classmates and I were no longer little kids. We were serious students competing for grades, for boys, and for glory. As for me, I wanted glory. I had sought to be the president of every organization I was involved in. I was more interested in glory than anything else. Perhaps it was to compensate for being poor.

"Whatever the reason, my pursuit of glory had made my grades slip; I wasn't even on the top ten list anymore. So when I decided to prove my father wrong for thinking I'd never amount to anything, I knew I had to do something different; I had to drop out of the race for glory and join the race for grades.

"I started waking up at 4:00 am to study and I gave up my social life. When my friends got together for parties, I stayed home to study. My teachers noticed my daily performance improving but told me it was too late to raise my overall grades, since we were already on the last grading period and my previous grades were so low.

"Perhaps they did not want to raise my expectations in case I got disappointed, but I closed my ears to their low expectations, much like I had to my dad. I continued to work hard and when our final grades were computed, I surprised my teachers, classmates, and best of all, my Dad. I was back on the top ten list and I'd made the third honor roll... thanks to my father's put-downs! This little piece of my life story reminds me of Romans 8:28 which says 'All things work together for good.' Indeed, even bad things can produce good results. For me, it was his discouraging words which encouraged me to raise my grades.

"Looking back, now I know that starting well in a race is important, but where we are in the end is what really matters. I believe this is true in our spiritual lives as well. We're all in a race! And our race requires us to focus on the prize by walking in the Spirit, so that we will not fulfill the desires of the flesh *(Galations 5:16)*.

"Like Paul, who had his focus on a higher goal when he said, 'My only aim is to finish the race and complete the task the Lord Jesus has given me the talk of testifying to the goodness of God's grace' *(Acts 20:24)*. As for me, I had my focus on proving that my father was wrong."

Chapter 9

NEED FOR BEAUTY AND GRACE

"So you ended up doing well," remarked Aunt Julia. "That's strange, I don't remember you graduating from high school in Mankayan?"

"No, I didn't," I confirmed. "I wanted to get away from my father so I went to Manila to live with my sister Marie. That's where I finished high school. I was so excited when I was told I'd be going to a private school. I thought it would give me the best education. But it didn't; on the contrary, it gave me the worst!

"I was so disappointed when my new classmates told me that only the three smartest students in the class studied and everyone else just copied their work. But my disappointment subsided when I realized that it was really to my advantage. I had my sister's kids to watch after school and a boyfriend to entertain, so I really didn't have time to study. I settled with copying my classmates' work. The only thing I got from that school was my diploma and that was fine with me since it was all I needed to get into college.

"Doing nothing during my last year of high school, however, caught up with me in college. I could not do algebra at all! Fortunately, my professor took pity on me and gave me a 'C.' I felt awful because I knew I didn't deserve it. She could have failed me but she did not. Back then I didn't have a word for what she did, but later I found out that it's called 'grace.'

"I found it in Titus 2:11, 'For the grace of God has appeared that brings salvation to all men.' The word of God taught me that concept of grace comes from God who put grace into action by sending His Son, Jesus Christ, to die for us even though we didn't deserve His sacrifice. Simply put, I learned that grace is God giving us a gift through Jesus Christ who died for all of us sinners who do not deserve His love. However, unless we accept His gift, we cannot benefit from it. I would not have benefited from my professor's gift had I not humbly received it from her. Honestly, I was embarrassed to receive the grade but I had to take it because I didn't want to repeat the subject and prolong my misery in Algebra.

"Another wonderful thing about my professor's grace was that it made me do something with it. It encouraged me to pass it on. When I became an instructor myself, I passed the same grace on to some engineering students who struggled in my English class since I knew they did not need to master English grammar and parts of speech to excel in their careers.

"However, unlike God, whose grace is inclusive, my grace was exclusive. I only gave grace to people I liked. I denied grace to my father, much like the unforgiving debtor in Matthew 18. In this story, the debtor was given grace by his master who forgave him and set him free so he didn't have to go to prison for his debt. But instead of doing the same thing for his co-worker, who owed him less money, this debtor sent him to prison. Like the master in the story, God gave me mercy by not giving me the punishment I deserved. I deserved penalty for my sins, but God gave me forgiveness instead. He also gave me love and grace that I did not deserve. Yet I withheld that grace from my own father.

"My bitterness over my father's view of me as the ugliest of his children lingered into my adulthood and remained unsettled until his death." I stopped, feeling like I may have said too much. I wasn't sure I even wanted to go on with the story about my father.

"Go on," Aunt Julia prodded. Her facial expression at that moment, however, made me cautious about what I was about to say and how I would say it, lest I be misunderstood.

Suddenly, an inspiring picture of a frog that I had seen years ago came to mind and gave me just the springboard I needed. "Let me tell you something first!" I said, and began to tell them about the frog incident.

"It was my first year of teaching in Tennessee when this happened. One of my co- teachers wanted to talk to my students, so I left the room and stood in the corridor. While standing there, I noticed a picture of a giant frog on the wall that I'd never noticed before. This frog was loaded with warts of all sizes. There was only one word you could use to describe this frog: UGLY. However, underneath the picture, there was a verse written in bold letters that changed everything. The verse said, 'I will praise you, for I am fearfully and wonderfully made!' It was Psalms 139:14.

"After my encounter with this ugly frog, my confidence in my appearance swelled. I started to see myself the way God sees me; as a daughter who is beautifully and wonderfully made! It taught me how God sees each of His children.

"The frog isn't what kept me from being negatively affected by my father's perception of me when I was younger, however. I'd already established in my mind that I was not as ugly as he thought because the boys at school who liked me were handsome." I grinned and Ruth and Louisa giggled.

"Their grades were not high because they would rather play, but they were handsome. Sadly, although Dad's perception of me did not affect the way I viewed myself, it became the issue that tore us apart. I tried to fix it, but I failed.

"Hang on," said Ruth, "you need to pause because I need a rest room break." I stood up, so she could leave the table easily. As soon as she came back, I picked up where I'd left off.

Chapter 10

SILENT FIGHT WITH FATHER AND MY REGRET

"DURING MY FIRST YEAR OF teaching at Philippines Christian University, I decided to start visiting my parents. This meant more than a day of travel for me. On one of my visits, my uncle and cousins were there, too. That evening, I was enjoying the fresh, cool air at an open bedroom window when my cousin came close to me and whispered, 'I do not understand your dad; every time you come home, all you ever say is: *I am going to buy this for my father*. I never hear you say, *I am going to buy this for my mother*. And yet your dad still says you are the ugliest of all his children! My sister overheard him saying it to my father.'

"I was shocked. I did not realize until that moment, that even at that stage of my life I was still trying to convince him I was someone beautiful, only this time I was using gifts.

"I though that I'd impressed him by finishing college without asking for a penny. I thought my sacrifice of going to see them and help them out would count for something beautiful. But it didn't. If he could have, my father would have remade me with the looks he wanted me to have. I could not understand why he felt it necessary to tell his brother, that night, he thought I was still single because of my looks. That night, I was angry; no, I was furious!

"I wondered whether my father had ever read I Samuel 16, where Samuel was trying to figure out who among Jesse's sons God would choose to replace Saul as king. Samuel was pretty sure it would be Eliab because of his physical appearance but God said, 'Do not look at his physical stature for the Lord does not see as man sees, for men look at the outward appearance but the Lord looks at the heart.'

"I lay down and tried to sleep but my thoughts swirled; *Dad is an avid reader. How in the world has he not learned that beauty is in the eye of the beholder?*

I certainly had. I had learned from experience that beauty depends on a person's perception. I'd once met a guy who was not attractive at all, but when I saw that girls were flocking to him, I had to find out why. I discovered that his secret was humility and a tender heart.

"Once that dawned on me, he became the most handsome man alive in my eyes and I wanted him to be friends with only me. When he realized that I was jealous of the other girls, he rebuked me for my selfishness. I was stunned by his rebuke but he was right and I was thankful he was brave enough to confront me. Otherwise, I may have never have recognized the sin I needed to deal with.

"So that night, as I tossed and turned in bed, I just couldn't understand why my dad couldn't see past my looks. *Was he not my father; my own flesh and blood? Where would my looks have come from if not from him? It's not my fault I look like his sibling who passed away.'* I complained to myself, *He is so unfair!*

"I debated with myself over how to respond. Love told me let it go. Prudence told me to be the better person. But human logic told me I'd be a fool to overlook such an offense, and my arrogance insisted that I should hold him responsible. I decided that he needed to be taught a lesson and that I should quit visiting him. The idea of teaching him to keep his opinions to himself sounded like the best choice and the more I thought about it, the more I was convinced that I was doing the right thing.

"I also realized that I hadn't been visiting my parents out of love, but out of a sense of duty. Going home had become a chore. Now I had the perfect reason to stop.

"Brazen with arrogance, I left my parents home the next morning without saying goodbye and vowed I'd never return.

"Looking back, I realize that I'd allowed my flesh to take over my decision-making. I did not take Paul's advice, 'Be angry, and do not sin; do not let the sun go down you on your wrath' *(Ephesians 4:26)*. Instead of letting the offense go before I went to sleep, I munched on it, savored it, and craved more of it until it twisted my sense of judgment. The wrong thing began to feel right and the right thing did not matter to me anymore.

"As I'd promised myself, I never went back; not until after I'd gotten the news that my father had died. That was when I felt the pain of my foolish decision.

"I was already living in the U.S., in Tennessee, when I got the news. The sad thing is, a few months prior, I'd already had a change of heart. I'd prayed that God would give me the chance to go home and make things right. I was willing to do whatever it took to iron things out between us.

"The hopelessness of never being able to make things right, and the guilt of not doing the right thing when I'd had the chance, crushed me to pieces. In agony I bawled, 'Forgive me God!' again and again until I was too exhausted to cry. It was awful.

"Yet even in my dire distress, I experienced God's forgiveness and comfort. I felt it the way it's described by Paul when he draws a distinction between godly sorrow and worldly sorrow: 'For godly sorrow produces repentance leading to salvation; not to be regretted, but the sorrow of the world produces death' *(2 Corinthians 6:10)*. In my hopelessness, He gave me hope; in my sadness, He gave me joy; in my anxiety, He gave me peace.

"Does this mean the pain was all over after that? Of course not! Satan would spring back up like the weeds I have to pull out of my flower garden. Once in while he still successfully takes me back to the scene where he'd equipped me with arrogance, selfishness, and perverted philosophy and then leaves me there to wallow in my guilt while he condemns me. But with God's word, I brush him off by reminding myself that God has already forgiven me and covered my sins with His blood, like it says in Romans 4:7. The Bible also says that 'as far as the east if from the west, so far has He removed my transgressions from me,' in Psalm 103:12. What a blessing it is to have a God who says, 'I even I, am the He who blots our your transgression for My own sake: I will not remember your sins' *(Isaiah 43:25)*.

Chapter 11

Chased by Fear but Finding Faith in Jesus

I'D TAKEN A BREAK FROM TELLING my story to eat a few more tortillas and finish my tea when Aunt Julia went back to a previous topic. "What about your fear of the dead, did you get over that?"

I nodded my head and responded, "Yes, but it was only after I'd read in the Bible that dead people don't have the power to hurt the living. That fear chased me from childhood till adulthood.

"I was in my first year of college at the Baguio Colleges Foundation when I realized that my fear was, in fact, getting worse. I avoided places where they held services for the dead and I couldn't be left alone in the dark. I was desperately looking for anything that would give me relief from that fear."

"Wait a minute!" interrupted Ruth when she saw the waiter carrying a jug of tea and called him to refill her glass. Then she motioned for me to go on.

"One Saturday morning, I was alone in the boarding house. My roommate had gone to visit her parents. I was sitting on my bed when a lady knocked on our door. Her name was Marcy and she'd come to visit my roommate, but since my roommate was gone I entertained her myself. While we were talking, she noticed my green Gideon New Testament Bible that was given to me in school. She asked if it was mine and if I'd already read it. I told her that I had tried but was frustrated because it was just a story being repeated over and over again. She told me that I did not understand my Bible because I didn't have the Holy Spirit yet.

"That got my attention! Marcy began by telling me that I first had to admit I was a sinner. She opened my Bible and had me read Romans 3:23 where it says, 'For all have sinned and fallen short of the glory of God.' Then she told me to repent of my sins and pray for Jesus to come into my heart to be my Savior and Lord.

"While she was talking, my heart was pounding. I was listening intently and trying to understand every word she said. Since I wasn't really sure how to do what she was telling me to do, she offered to lead me in a prayer in which I could repeat the words. As we prayed, I meant every word that came out of my mouth.

"Later, during one of my daily devotions, I found a passage of Scripture that described what I felt while Marcy was explaining the gospel to me. It was the story of the two men walking on the Road to Emmaus who were talking and walking with Jesus completely unaware of who He was: 'Did not our hearts burn within us while He talked with us on the road and while He opened the Scripture to us? *(Luke 24: 32)."*

"Marcy kept coming back to help me grow spiritually. She also introduced me to others who'd also accepted Christ. She made sure I understood God's message of salvation and helped me to establish a habit of daily Bible reading and prayer.

"The Bible became a vital part of my life after my encounter with Marcy. It became my source of knowledge in my search for truth. One day, I was reading in the book of Ecclesiastes when I come across the passage that says, 'For the living know that they will die, but the dead know nothing; and they have no more reward. For the memory of them is forgotten. Also, their love, their hatred, and their envy have not perished. Nevermore will they have a share in anything done under the sun' *(Ecclesiastes 9:5-6).*

"These verses brought me back to the feeling of being haunted by dead people back in seventh grade. I brooded over these verses and asked myself, 'If dead people do not take part in anything that is happening under the sun, why did I get well after my grandmother spoke to my dead aunt? Who was it that spoke with the voice of a man through a lady when my grandfather died?'

"I came to the conclusion that if the dead could not do any good or bad, then it must just be the devil playing tricks on those of us who believed in the power of the dead to make us sick or well.

"Armed with this conclusion, I decided to go back to Sagada to face my fears. Upon arrival at my grandmother's house, I told her that I wanted to sleep on the spot where my grandfather's coffin had been laid. Before I lay down, I told the devil that he could not scare me anymore because I had Jesus who was more powerful than he was. I started reading my Bible and when I got sleepy, I put the Bible on my chest and went to sleep. When I woke up, I read some more.

"I could feel the enemy trying to get a foothold and induce fear, but he was unsuccessful. I held on to my source of strength: Jesus. When morning came, the fight was over.

I smiled and said: 'See! I told you. You cannot scare me anymore!'

"That morning, I felt liberated! I was so excited! I had no more fear of the dead! When I left my grandmother's house that day, I had the utter confidence that I had overcome my fear of the dead and that things would be alright from then on."

Chapter 12

WINDING TOY AND RECONQUERING FEAR

"HERE COMES MORE FOOD!" I announced. The smell of the food took our attention away from the story and we eagerly dug in. When the excitement mellowed, Aunt Julia took me back, yet again, to the fear of the dead.

"So you were really able to totally overcome your fear of the dead?" she asked intently.

"Well, at that moment I did," I told her honestly, "and I was doing really well until the night I was tested again. I had gone to visit my Aunt Mercedes in Sta. Ana, Manila when one of her workers passed away. He was close to the family and had often hung around my Aunt's place. In fact, he had a seat reserved for himself that nobody else could use when he was there.

"I'd just arrived when I found that my aunt and everyone else had left to attend his funeral service. Finding myself alone, knowing they'd gone to visit the dead, gave me a creepy feeling. Before I knew it, the memories of how the devil scared me in the past came rushing back to me. I knew I had to fight that ghostly feeling, so I went over and sat right on that man's favorite seat and told the devil he couldn't fool me again.

"While I was speaking, my young cousins' toy, which needed to be wound in order to work, suddenly started playing from inside of a glass display cabinet. Knowing no-one had wound it, I immediately established that it was the devil trying to inflict fear on me again.

"I stood my ground and with all the spiritual strength I could muster, I again told the devil in a firm voice that he did not have any power over me anymore. In the past, I didn't have the 'sword of the Spirit, which is the Word of God' *(Ephesians 6:17)* to hold on to. I'd run to people instead.

"But this time, I stood up and told the devil a third time that he could not scare me anymore. I went to the bedroom, got the clothes I'd brought, and started doing the laundry. After washing my clothes, I believe the devil left because the creepy atmosphere was gone. Once more, I felt liberated. With this victory, I felt empowered.

"In bed that night, I wondered what would have happened if I'd entertained the fears. With gratitude, I smiled and went to sleep peacefully.

"When I woke up in the morning, I was thinking about what had happened when it suddenly occurred to me that my fears had not actually started in Sagada, back in seventh grade. I remembered that the year before, when I'd been living with Ms. Garcia, Janet and I would join her older sisters in their midnight gatherings playing a board game called 'Ouija board.' While I found it fascinating that the supposed spirit of the person they summoned could spell out answers to their questions, I also found it incapacitating and controlling. I was never able to sleep afterwards; after every game, I would lie awake imagining all the scary things the devil put into my little head. Unfortunately, I knew nothing then about this enemy that 'prowls like a roaring lion, seeking someone to devour' *(1 Peter 5:8)*.

"In fact, it was the Apostle Paul who explained the devil's invisibility, his power, and his co-workers to me. Paul said, 'For we wrestle not against flesh and blood, but against principalities, against powers, against the rulers of darkness of this age, against spiritual hosts of wickedness in the heavenly places' *(Ephesians 6:12)*. That was the worst thing about my enemy. I couldn't see him, yet he was controlling me through fear.

"Thankfully, the Bible did not just give me the warning about the enemy's power to control and destroy, but also gave me the key to withstanding him: "Finally, my brethren, be strong in the Lord and in the Power of His might. Put on the whole armor of God that you may be able to stand against the wiles of the devil.... Stand therefore, having girded your waist with truth, having put on the breastplate of righteousness, having shod your feet with the preparation of the gospel of peace, above all, taking the shield of faith with which you will be able to quench all the fiery darts of the wicked one. And take the helmet of salvation and the sword of the Spirit which is the Word of God; praying always with prayer and supplication in the Spirit '(Ephesians 6:10-18).

"Looking back, every time I failed, it was because I did not use the 'sword of the Spirit,' which is the Word of God. I often relied on my flesh to defensively fight my battle on my own instead of offensively standing up and using the armor of God.

Chapter 13

Faith that Moves Mountains and Gets Jobs

Aunt Julia settled back in her chair with a satisfied smile. I felt encouraged to tell her more about the faith I found after leaving Mankayan and about how I grew spiritually. I wanted to testify as to what faith in God can do.

"Spending time with God in His Word helped me experience 'faith that moves mountains' as described in Matthew 7:20. In the Bible, I saw God display His promises to provide for my needs and my faith grew bountifully. Now I fully believe that He delivers on His every Word.

"I didn't learn to trust Him all at once, though; my first experience in trusting Him to provide for my needs happened in a very unusual way. It was a Sunday morning and I'd left the Manila Bible Seminary to go to a church somewhere. That trip took two rides: a tricycle and a jeepney. When I got down from the tricycle at my stop, I realized that I only had enough coins to pay the tricycle driver. I'd forgotten my wallet and only had leftover coins in my bag. I was stuck! I had no money to go back, and I couldn't go forward.

"I had to think. I did not want to beg because I had my Sunday dress on so I was pretty sure no-one would believe my story." The women nodded in understanding.

"Then I realized that I had to pray. So I stood on the side of the road and prayed, 'God, You told me that You would provide for all that I need. I need you to help me right now.'

"After I prayed, I took the first empty jeepney. Right after I got on, I noticed two coins that a previous passenger had dropped.

I recognized immediately that the coins were the exact amount that I needed. I picked them up and gave them to the driver. I smiled and thanked God. That was my first taste of God's miraculous provision.

"My second test in trusting His provision took place when I'd just finished my BA in English at Philippine Christian University. I graduated in October, which wasn't a good time to hunt for a job, but I'd prayed fervently for God to give me a job and was confident that He would. Meanwhile, to keep busy, I went to enroll in the masters' degree program and had barely left the registrar when I noticed the English Department secretary running towards me and shouting excitedly, despite the other students around. He announced that the school next to us, Philippine Women's University, needed a teacher and I was the one the department wanted to endorse!

"I jumped in jubilation and said, 'Yes, that is mine! Thank you God, for answering my prayer so quickly!'

"I wish it went as smoothly as I thought it would, but it did not. What I was not aware of was that there were two of us who'd applied for the job. Right after we'd given our teaching demos, the principal told me that there was a big difference between English and Education majors. Needless to say, they needed someone with an Education degree and I was not it.

"However, the peace I felt when she told me the news was beyond my comprehension; I was not disappointed! I was not ashamed or discouraged. It was amazing! I simply had this quiet peace that assured me that everything was going to be all right. I smiled as I thanked her; I did not get the job, but I was rejoicing! I was even singing on my way back home. I was not sure why, but God's joy was just bubbling up within me.

"Two days later, I got a call from the University to report to work. I laughed and thanked God for the way He worked things out. I never found out what happened to the lady who'd been offered the job. My best guess was that God gave her a job closer to her home. But there was something I was confident of: the job was given to me by God.

"My third test came when I arrived in Tennessee. When I applied to get a teaching certificate, I was required to turn in all the documents proving my education since I'd come from a different country. That was the easy part. The hard part was overcoming my husband Joe's doubts that I would ever be hired to teach English because I'd only learned it as a second language. My husband was not alone in his opinion. Though they did not verbally express their incredulity, the expressions on our friends' faces did. Their skepticism did not really bother me, but Joe's doubt did. While I agreed with their logic, I did not agree in my heart.

"In contrast, I believed that God did not bring me to the U.S. to stop using the education He'd allowed me to accomplish. I never doubted that God was going to use me as a teacher when the right time came. With this conviction, I was able to ward off discouragement. In the meantime, I knew I had to prepare myself for the job. My past experience taught me that before God could use me, I had to be prepared; I had to be equipped with whatever was necessary to make it happen.

"So the first thing I did was convince my husband to allow me to go to the University and stay in one of their apartments. It was an hour away from our home and I wanted to live there until I'd finished all the requirements to get a teaching certificate. Of course, his first answer was a big fat 'NO!' I knew that would be his response. In fact, I expected it. However, his reaction did not stop me from continuing to pray and believe it was going to happen. I did not fight back or argue. I patiently waited for God and His timing.

"Finally, that day arrived! How did that happen? Well, one day, I told Joe that if I met God face to face and He asked me why I did not use my profession, I would tell Him that my husband did not allow me to get a teaching certification. That must have changed his mind because he did not just allow me to go, he helped me move into the apartment, paid all of my school expenses, and lived sacrificially alone to help me reach my goal. God made him favorable toward me. From then on, every time my husband said 'no' to what I was asking, I used the same strategy. And it always worked!

"Since our home was surrounded by elementary schools, I decided to get an elementary teaching certification. After successfully attaining one, I taught elementary school for eight years. Then I applied to teach English as a Second Language at Roane State College. RSC was just a five minute drive from where we lived. I had prayed, years prior, to someday be able to teach at this college.

"While I was applying, I was confronted with the issue of disbelief again. This time, it was not my husband, but my co-teacher and very good friend who had doubts. What confused me was that she'd recommended me, and yet she doubted I was going to get the job. Contrary to her skepticism, I was sure I was going to get hired because God had always given me the 'desire of my heart.' Psalms 37:4 is the verse that I'd memorized, believed, and claimed every time I prayed for something good.

"I did end up getting the ESL job at Roane State College under their continuing education program. Then I moved on to teach the same subject for Roane County Adult Education, as well as teaching some GED classes.

"'Nothing is impossible with God' from Luke 1:37 has always been my bulwark against pessimism. Clinging tightly to what God can do keeps me from being influenced by people's doubts. Yes, there were times when my faith wavered, but when it did, all I had to do was to recall those days when He miraculously provided the coins that I needed, or gave me my first teaching job, or changed my husband's heart so I could get my certification, or gave me the opportunity to teach English.

"Reminiscing over all of my answered prayers as well as His countless blessings, both big and small, makes me spring back up fully charged to thank Him, praise Him, and trust Him some more!"

Chapter 14

MEETING JOE

LAUGHTER BROKE OUT NEAR US as a group of friends were taking selfies. We thought it was a good idea and stopped to take a few pictures of our own. When we were finished, I showed them Joe's picture on my cell phone. As my phone was passed around, Ruth asked, "How did you meet your husband?"

"Yes, that was one of my questions!" Aunt Julia seconded. I smiled, and with excitement, began to tell them the most exciting part of my life.

"Well, it all began when I was taking a speech class at Philippine Christian University. Our speech teacher told us that if we really wanted to enhance our ability to speak English, we needed to speak with native English speakers. I went home thinking about it and mentioned it to my sister Annie who'd just arrived from Taiwan. The next thing I knew I was receiving all kinds of mail from the U.S.!

"In short, my husband was one of my male pen pals. In his first letter, he got straight to the point. He told me he was looking for a wife. I was already nearly finished with my master's degree, so at the time my next goal was to get married. I had actually started praying for a husband just before his letter arrived. In response to his letter, I asked him four questions: 'Do you smoke? Do drink alcohol? Do you gamble? Do you believe in God?'

"And he answered: 'No, I don't smoke. No, I don't drink alcohol. No, I don't gamble. Yes, I believe in God.' And then he posed his own question: 'Are you a Christian?'

"I was happy to get the answers I was hoping for, so we started writing back and forth and sending pictures to each other. When mail seemed too slow, we decided to use the phone. Luckily for me, I was already at school by the time he called, so he had to pay all the bills. After ten months, he decided to come to the Philippines to see me.

"When I got his message, I got anxious. I was not really 100 percent sure he was the 'God-sent' one, so I prayed, "God, if he is the one let him come, and if he is not, please stop him because I don't want him to travel halfway around the world only to go home disappointed."

"Then the phone rang. He told me he already had his plane ticket! With that, I knew in my heart that he was the one. When we met at the airport for the first time, we felt like we'd known each for a long time. So that night when he asked me to marry him, my response was: 'Of course!' The following day, we started processing our papers."

Ruth and Louisa were open-mouthed with surprise. I grinned, "Yep, it went that quick! When I arrived in Tennessee, I wanted to see the Christian Singles Magazine where Joe had found my name. To my surprise, all I found was a three-sentence description of me! It was written in tiny letters and would have been easy to overlook because it was surrounded by photos of so many pretty ladies. I asked him why he had chosen me when I did not even have a picture attached to my description. Joe said it was because he liked what I wrote.

"It made me feel secure to know that he valued what I had inside me, but I just had to know if I was actually beautiful to him. So I asked him bluntly, 'Honey, am I beautiful?'

"He responded, 'Of course you're beautiful! I wouldn't have married you if you weren't.' Throughout our married life, I asked that question over and over and I am glad he always gave me the same response.

"We were married for almost 25 years before Joe died of cancer. I would say that he was the best husband in the world. Did we have problems in our marriage? Of course! We had them in spades. I would be lying if I said it was always hunky-dory."

Chapter 15

BEING A PROFESSIONAL DRIVER IN THE US

Louisa must have dropped something on the floor because she ducked her head under the table and when she popped back up, she asked, "What was the greatest challenge in being married to a foreigner?"

"Well," I responded, "I thought our cultural differences would be the greatest challenge, but they were not. It wasn't a personality difference, either. It turns out, the things we had to grapple with were anger and arrogance. I had more of those things than he did. Our marriage revealed the worst in me. I hadn't realized how short-tempered and arrogant I was. I held on to past mistakes instead of letting them go. Incredibly, my husband did not run away from me!

"Did you ever have big fights?" asked Ruth.

"Yes, but they were not loud. They were short because neither of us wanted to prolong the misery of misunderstanding. Our first and worst fight happened when my husband started teaching me how to drive. Being a careful driver, he was a nervous wreck when he saw the slightest chance of danger while I was driving. He would scream, which made me a more reckless driver. As a result, I almost killed him three times during our driving practice!"

Ruth and Louisa bust out laughing. "What happened then?" asked Aunt Julia.

"Finally, I had it! I asked, 'Why don't you hire someone to teach me how to drive?' And he answered, 'Why would I hire someone to teach you something that I already know?'"

"And that settled it. I knew then that I would have to practice on my own; otherwise, our fights would just last longer.

"One afternoon, while he was taking a nap, I sneaked out to practice. What I did not take into account was how the soil on the side of the road had softened up because it had been raining. My right rear wheel got caught in the mud and stuck. I could not move forward or backward so I had to walk back home to wake Joe up from his sweet little nap. To my surprise, he did not get mad. He just took his tractor and tried to pull my car out. But the chain snapped and my car went rolling down the hill. As we watched it roll away, my husband cried, 'There goes your car!'

Ruth and Louisa broke into incredulous laughter. I giggled along with them and continued, "He didn't speak to me for two days, and I dared not say anything either. I thought our marriage was over! Surprisingly, that freak accident turned out to be a blessing! The insurance company gave us more money than my car was worth, so we were able to buy a better one.

"Getting a license was a totally different ball game. I could not wait to have my license so Joe took me to take the test. But my first instructor was worse than my husband. As soon as we left DMV – that's the Department of Motor Vehicles – parking lot, she started screaming at me and didn't stop until we came back. In a loud, angry voice she told Joe not to bring me back until I had plenty of practice.

"I thought Joe was going to be angry, but instead, he just laughed loudly as if it was the funniest thing in the world!" This set all of the women giggling again.

"A month after that, he drove us six hours to go visit my sister Emily in Memphis. Joe told my sister what happened and my sister told us to try the test there in Memphis because the instructors were lenient. We took her advice and went. I still did not pass, but my sister was right. My instructor was very calm and encouraging. She told me all I needed was a little more practice. She even said I could come back the next day, and I would surely pass the test. What she did not tell me was that the following day was a holiday. Joe and I giggled at *having* being tricked as he drove us back home.

"I finally got my license on the third try. As soon as I got my license, I refused to drive when Joe was with me. One day, he expressed his curiosity. 'When you did not have a license, you want to drive all the time. Now that you have a license, why do you not want to drive?'

"I explained, 'I am now a professional driver! I do not want to be hollered at anymore!' He laughed, and that was my rule from then on.

"I believe this was the worst fight we faced as married couple. After we got through this one, the rest of our disagreements were not bad all. I believe that our faith in God and faith that our marriage was going to last with His help, played an important role in our relationship. We both wanted to please the Lord. That was the glue that held us together. We strove to achieve the unity that Paul encouraged: 'I...beseech you to walk worthy of your calling with which you were called, with all lowliness and gentleness, with longsuffering, bearing with one another in love, endeavoring to keep the unity of the Spirit in the bond of peace' *(Ephesians 4:1-3)*.

"Were we always successful? Certainly not! But God always gave us reasons to overlook each other's differences in order to achieve reconciliation in the shortest time possible. That was how we faced every challenge that posed to tear us apart. And as we grew older, our relationship became sweeter and stronger until we came to the realization that we had reached spiritual unity: we were no longer two but one.

Chapter 16

GOING BACK TO THE THING ABOUT MY NAME

THE LAUGHTER INSIDE THE restaurant got louder. I took a look around and realized the restaurant was packed. *It's like we're having a contest to see who can talk the loudest,* I thought. As soon as I turned back to the table, Louisa said, 'I didn't get a chance to ask earlier; who told you that your name means pain and sorrow?'

"I can't remember who told me what it means," I replied, "but when I was learning Spanish and had the chance to mingle with

Spanish people, I was told that 'Dolor' means 'a pain' and 'Dolores' means 'many pains.'

"No wonder that even as a child I disliked my name – even when I did not know what it meant![4] I think even my friends disliked it because everywhere I went, I received a new nickname: Ambit, Dolly, Dee, Little D, Doyet...

"'Ambit' was the name given to me as a little girl. It made me feel light and small. 'Dolor' is what my family calls me. I guess they wanted to shorten it to lessen the 'curse.' My grandparents called me 'Doroles,'" I smiled, "and so did anyone else who couldn't pronounce 'Dolores.'

---

[4] I knew from experience that it is horrible to have a name that makes people laugh at you. I understood that very clearly. That is why when I had a student with last name 'Panti,' I deeply empathized because every time I called roll I could hear waves of giggles. I would always sit up straighter and give my students a serious look as my way of saying, 'stop!' I really wished there was something I could do to help her, but at time, I couldn't think of anything to say that would help. After that semester, I never had her again in any of my classes, but the memory of her lingers because we had a similar problem.

'Dolly' was the nickname given to me by my co-teachers during my first year at Philippine Women's University. They were trying to make my name sound classy because they thought it was too old fashioned. Later, when I moved to Tennessee and was teaching at the jail, one of my students jokingly told me I looked like Dora the Explorer with my short, black bob and big backpack. From then on, I was called 'Dora' by some of the inmates and officers.

"Of all my nicknames, though, Doyet is the one I like best because of the way it came about. One evening, during our devotion time at the Manila Bible Seminary, my dorm mother called and told me that her friend, whose name was 'Yet,' had not arrived to help her sing a song. She had a beautiful voice and wanted me to sing with her. After our song, she announced that, from then on, my name would be 'Doyet' because I was her friend's replacement. I became 'Doyet' to everyone overnight.

"But God really has a way of redeeming my name for me. My music teacher, Mrs.

Hale, made me realize how beautiful 'Dolores' actually sounds. One day, she was calling me at the top of her voice to get my attention before I left.

"'Do-lo-res!' She sounded like she was singing the solfege – you know, 'do-re-me-fa-so-la-ti-do.' It was so magical to hear! With my hands covering my gaping mouth, I thought, *Is that me?* Of course it was me! From then on, I started taking pride in my name and wanted to be called Dolores. Mrs. Hale made me love my name.

"Later in life, again as I was reading the Bible, I discovered a person who had the same problem. But his relationship with God gave him the confidence to ask for something that made him more honorable than all his brothers.

"His name was Jabez. In 1 Chronicles, chapter four tells the story of a mother who named her son Jabez because she birthed him in pain. This little story simply says that Jabez prayed and said, 'Oh, that you would bless me indeed, and enlarge my territory, that Your hand would be with me, and that You would keep me from evil, that I may not cause pain!' From his last phrase, I deem that he suffered pain as well. Though I'm not sure if it was related to his name, I believe he suffered pain because his last request was that he would not cause pain. I believe he was referring to the same kind of pain that had been inflicted on him. So I admire this guy because he didn't want others to experience it, and he made sure he wouldn't be the source of such pain. No wonder God granted his request.

"It wasn't until I moved to the Tennessee that I finally had the chance to be called 'Dolores' by everyone. I was no longer bothered by what it meant, even if my Spanish friends sometimes teased me about it. I reminded myself that I had been washed, sanctified, and justified in the name of the Lord Jesus Christ and by the Spirit of God' *(1 Corinthians 6:11)*. I was a 'new creation.' The old had gone and the new had come *(2 Corinthians 5:17)*. I am not a slave of pain, nor am I a pain to others any longer; I'm a slave of righteousness. I am Dolores, a child of God."

Chapter 17

THE DESIRE TO LEARN SPANISH AND GO TO THE MISSION FIELD BY FAITH

"Is that what inspired you to learn Spanish?" asked Ruth, "Your name?"

"I never thought of that," I answered. "All I know is that one summer, in Tennessee, when the school's Spanish teacher decided to return home to Texas, I realized that our school would need someone to take her place. I spent the whole summer learning Spanish on the computer, using all the free lessons I could find. Fortunately for me, all I had to learn was Spanish grammar because Spanish and Tagalog have the same phonics. When we returned to school, I asked the principal, Dr. Brenda Murphy, if she would let me teach the Spanish class so I could continue to learn while I taught.

"To my surprise, she said, 'Of course Dolores,' and it was official. I was the new Spanish teacher. My after-school students who were really interested in learning Spanish were so happy with the class that they stayed with me for four years. What they did not know was that I was just a page ahead of them every time they came to class!"

Ruth chuckled and I continued, "Then one night, I was awakened by the thought, *Why do I have this insatiable desire to learn Spanish?*

"I could not go back to sleep, so I got up and went to my computer. As I sat there, I wondered if I was supposed to go to the mission field; to a Spanish-speaking country to teach English as a second language. So I searched 'ESL teacher abroad' and in a flash,

I got an overwhelming number of organizations needing ESL teachers!

"My desire to go shot through the roof and my heart started pounding. I kept repeating, 'This is it! This is it!' It did not take me long to decide I would go. I chose the International School Project because it reminded me of Campus Crusade for Christ, the organization that had exposed me to evangelism when I was in college. I thought it was time for me to do something in return.

"When my husband and I were having breakfast the following morning, I told him I was going on a short term mission trip to Guatemala and that I needed three thousand dollars for it. Joe was so surprised he didn't say anything. The following day, I told him again. Finally, he responded, 'Where are you going to get that money?'

"Ah! It was the money he was worried about! I was confident God would provide it because I was sure He was the One giving me the desire. When I am confident that my desire is something good and aligns with God's plan, I believe He will provide what I need and equip me to do it. So in response, I said, 'I will raise my own support.' I guess that was something new to him because all he did was shake his head.

"The first thing I did was call seven ladies to pray for me so that someone would pray with me each day. On the seventh day, which was Sunday, I talked to our pastor and told him about the mission trip to Guatemala. I told him I needed to raise $3000 in one month. He announced it to our church that very afternoon.

"'Dolores is going to Guatemala on a mission trip,' he said, 'and she needs $3000. She isn't asking us to provide all of it; she is just asking if the church can help.'

"Jamey, our organist, raised his hand and asked, 'Why can't we give it all? We have the money.' Until that moment, I'd never realized how much respect and authority he carried in our church. His voice was soft, yet powerful, and the church was silence for a moment before – suddenly – everyone agreed! It was amazing; it felt like the money just fell into my lap. In quiet jubilation, I whispered, 'Thank you God!'

"Joe pressed my hand to express his 'Unbelievable!' response. My husband had witnessed what faith can do. From then on, he never questioned or opposed me again about anything that I wanted to do by faith, regardless of how far-fetched it seemed to him.

"Wait...I take that back. Though he didn't oppose what I wanted to do anymore, he still doubted my decisions sometimes. When I was working at the Morgan Correctional Complex as a GED and ESL teacher for Spanish students, I decided to apply for training credits to go to Honduras for Spanish Immersion. Though I knew that this was never done, I was confident that my application would be approved, so I told my husband about it.

"Of course, his reaction was, 'You can't do that!' I didn't tell anyone else so that I wouldn't hear any more negative responses before it was approved. I believe his faith grew as he watched me achieve anything I believed was going happen by faith.

The following year, when I told him I put in an application to go to Puerto Rico for Spanish immersion, his response was, 'When?' What a shift!

Chapter 18

"Your work place is your mission field."

Ruth asked a question I could not understand because she was distracted by a beautiful young woman walking toward us. When the woman got to our table, she pulled out a seat and sat right down. I looked at Ruth for explanation and she said, "Dolores, this is my daughter. Her name is Julie Ruth. She is a doctor."

"Oh, hello!" I said with a smile, "I'm glad you were able to join us!"

After she'd greeted everyone, I asked Ruth, "What was your question, again?"

"Oh, I was just wondering whether you ever got scared working in a prison."

"Hmm… not really. Maybe because I never went to work without making sure that God was with me. Everyday I remembered what a friend told me: 'Your work place is your mission field.' This friend was a missionary in Honduras who I'd asked to pray for me because I was applying to work in a penitentiary full of male inmates. He helped me to see that working there had spiritual value. I fully understand what he meant after I began teaching at the Morgan Country Correctional Complex.

"At the beginning, my husband didn't like the idea of me working in a prison. To be honest, I wasn't sure I wanted to work there either, so I prayed. My friend Charlene, who'd encouraged me to apply for the job, made it sound like it was the best place to work. Though I was excited at the idea, I was also apprehensive that I might fail. I was reminded of Moses, who reasoned with God about his inability to talk when He told him to go to

"Your work place is your mission field."

Egypt to tell Pharaoh to let His people go so that they could worship Him *(Exodus 9:1)*.

"I told my fears to God and asked that if it was His will for me to get the job, I would pass the interview. And once again, God humored me. I was so tickled to find out from Charlene 30 minutes after the interview that I'd gotten the job because the other applicant did not show up." I paused and then with a smile added, "I guess I really never found out whether I passed the interview or not. All I could do was thank Him over and over again as we drove home.

"I felt like the job was dropped from heaven just for me... but boy, my first day at school was wild! When Mike, the supervisor who walked me into the school, and I got inside the building, I saw an inmate down on the floor screaming and trying to fight off four officers!" I glanced at Aunt Julie and she looked horrified.

"But I found out later that he had a mental problem and they couldn't figure out how he'd gotten into that part of the building. I was glad they had me shadow for two weeks before my first day of teaching. My first day in the classroom was terrifying: someone threw an apple over my head and it splattered all over the wall behind me! I had to call the guards in to investigate and they told me it was likely intended for my teacher's aide, who they hated, and not for me.

"I was scared. I wasn't sure I could survive in that environment. But God had sent someone there ahead of me to help me overcome my fear, to give me advice, and to teach me how to deal with inmates. Her name was Julia. When she talked, the inmates listened. I was so impressed. I was not able to learn everything she taught me, but I learned enough to survive in such a challenging school setting

"Remembering my prayer partner's statement that the prison was my mission field, I made sure I was spiritually prepared to go to school every day. I would sing a song, memorize a verse, and pray a prayer of praise, thanksgiving and supplication. When I walked down the boulevard, I would sing and praise and pray. Before my students arrived, I would pray for all them and for the other workers.

"Your work place is your mission field."

In between classes, when I was in the conference room, which was also our dining room, I would sing with no regard for whether others wanted to hear a song or not. And when I couldn't finish a song, my co-teacher Lou Ann would finish it for me because she knew that I only knew the chorus to every song I sang.

"Those are the good memories, and oh how I love to remember them, but truthfully, what taught me the most were the bad memories. The ones I have to remember lest I repeat the same mistakes. Indeed, there were many of them, but the worst one was when I hurt my friend Julia, the one who had generously helped me. She said something that made me feel like she didn't care about my students, but instead of asking her what she meant, I took it cynically and let it fester in my mind the whole night. When I woke up in the morning, I was so angry I reported her to the principal. When Julia confronted me, I immediately realized that I'd made a mistake and I felt awful. I apologized, but it was not enough to fix our relationship. It looked like our friendship was broken over a lack of communication, but I discovered it was more than that. It was my own arrogance that caused the division.

"I believe this is what Paul meant when he warned his audience: 'Therefore let him who thinks he stands take heed lest he fall *(1 Corinthians 10:12).*' I was so confident I'd heard and understood Julia correctly during that afternoon meeting that it skewed my perspective.

Another consequence was that Julia had slept well that night while I stayed awake with my cynical thoughts. As a result, I fell. Proverbs 16:18 describes it well: 'Pride goes before destruction and haughty spirit before a fall.' She later forgave me and started helping me again before I retired, and for that I was thankful. While I treasure all the happy memories, I am thankful for the bad ones as well because of what I learned from them. My friend Charlene was right; it really was a good place to work."

Chapter 19

BEING THANKFUL IN TIMES OF TROUBLE

THE WOMEN WERE REFLECTIVE for a moment. And then Aunt Julia gently asked her last question. "When did you lose your husband?"

"Toward the end of 2017," I responded, "my husband got diagnosed with Mesothelioma cancer. When he told me that he wanted to live and that we might lose everything we owned in order for him to get well, I knew I had to back him up.

"We didn't waste any time. We flew immediately to Texas to find a hospital that dealt with that kind of cancer. When we arrived at MD Anderson hospital, Joe broke down for the first time. He cried and asked me to help him. It broke me to pieces, but I knew I had to be strong for him. Though I felt helpless myself, I had to assure him that I was there for him.

"One day, while I was waiting for Joe, I wondered how we would be able to get around without a car since we didn't know anyone in the area. To my amazement, we were welcomed by people who didn't know us, yet somehow understood how we felt and what we were going through. We found God's favor everywhere we went! We couldn't help but be thankful for how God was taking care of our needs. The hospital was full of sick people but it was also full of workers who were kind and loving to us. I was so impressed by how well they were taking care of the patients. Though our hearts were heavy, we strongly felt God's love, care and provision.

"The second time we went back to Texas for Joe's treatment, we met new people there who surprised us with their goodness. It was even better than the first time. Someone we did not know had volunteered to pick us up from the airport and take us to our apartment. When we arrived at the apartment, another volunteer offered us a trip to the grocery store. I called them angels because that was what they were to me. Hebrews 1:14 describes angels as 'ministering spirits sent to serve those who will inherit salvation.' Those people were not spirits, but I believe they were ministers sent by God to help us and others who needed them.

"Being in Texas with people who were there for the same reason we were gave us the opportunity to help and be helped. We dined with them and had fellowship with them. We prayed with them and cried with them. Together, we believed that our only hope was in God and that God was good. We all knew that whatever the results were, they were God's answer to our prayers. I believed that our experience there prepared Joe to accept whatever God had in store for him. After three months of living in Texas so Joe could finish all his treatments, we were told to return home for him to rest and that he should come back in three months for a checkup. We were also given the assurance that he was going to get well.

"However when Joe went back for his checkup expecting good news, he received bad news instead. Instead of getting bitter, though, he drove back home from Texas energized with a positive attitude. His best friend was with me at home waiting for him to arrive. When he opened the door, he was smiling to cheer up his best friend. He didn't cry, he didn't complain, he didn't blame anyone for what was happening to him. Instead, he talked about how short life is, how uncertain, and how the most important thing for us to do is to be ready when God calls us home.

"I thought he was going to cry after his friend left, but he maintained that positive attitude. He spent the rest of his days looking for opportunities to witness. He even called a friend in Florida to talk to him about God, about dying, and about the salvation that God gives to those who receive him. Because of his positive spiritual outlook, my husband became an encouragement to those who came over to encourage him.

"A lot had changed in Joe's heart since back when we'd first started praying that God would extend his life. Just like Hezekiah in 2 Kings 20:1-6, who cried and begged God to give him an extension of life, we did that too. However, while we were praying for healing to be God's will for Joe, God was doing a work in Joe's heart. I believe God aligned Joe's will with His.

"What happened to Joe reminds me what happened to David when he was praying for the survival of his son in 2 Samuel 12. He was described as laying on the ground pleading and fasting for his son to survive. But when he was informed that his son had died, he immediately got up and started eating. That's exactly how Joe reacted after he received the news that there was nothing they could do to cure him. He gracefully accepted it as God's will and believed it to be something better than the healing we'd asked for. Joe was at peace.

"Because of his gracious acceptance of the verdict, we were able to plan his funeral together and he was able to choose what clothes to wear, who was going to preach in the church, the songs that we would sing, even the color of his coffin. While he was doing these things, all I could see in Joe's face was confidence in God's promise to take him to a place where there's no more sorrow and no more tears *(Revelation 21:4)*. In fact, after he died, I discovered a story that he wrote about how God had His hand on him. It revealed what God had done for him that he had never told anyone about, including me, for reasons he alone knew."[5]

God's Hand on Me

When I was 6 months old, my Dad died from poison they used in the orange groves in Lake Placid, FL. His name was Cecil Pendarvis and that left my mother who could not take care of me. My grandmother, uncle Jerry's mother, had a cousin

---

[5] I did not show Joe's story to my friends the day of our dinner because I did not have it with me, but I am including it here, just as he wrote it.

named Mary married to Joseph Bennett who lived in Screven Georgia. Mary and Joseph lost three babies. I think one was born dead and the other two lived a year or so and died. Mary had an older son by previous marriage whose name was Bill Lord. I think Bill got married to Sara in 1949, the same year I was born. Mary was 41 and Joseph was 42. They had given up on having any more babies, but they wanted one very much. Joseph Bennett was a farmer on a 315 acres in Screven when they heard about the cousin's son's death and a baby boy needing a home. My grandparents were very poor. They had two kids, a daughter named Neil and a son named Jerry, so they could not raise me. That is how I ended up with Mary and Joseph Bennett. That was the **first time that God touched my life**. I was 6 months old. He gave me a Daddy and Momma that loved me. They took me to Church every Sunday to learn about Jesus. We were very happy. They spoiled me in some ways. My Daddy worked at the farm and drove a school bus while my Momma and Aunt Sara worked at shirt factory in Jesup about 15 miles away.

The next two events where **God's hand was on me** happened when I was 5 or 6 years old. I don't remember which came first. They were gathering tobacco, and I was too small to help, but I went out there toward the middle of the rows and fell asleep. The mule pulling the sled stepped on my foot. Thank God! It could have been on my stomach or something that could have caused death. No more than a year later, we all were swimming in our pond that the county dug, a nice size pond, about 60 feet wide by 200 feet long. It was very deep in some places but not so deep in some spots. It had a ridge under the water about 2 or 3 feet from the top where the drag line missed places that made it the same deep. I was playing in the shallow place where everybody else was. I had a swimmie float on my back, but took it off, I guess because I was the only one with one. I was playing around and found the ridge and started walking on it. Well, I slipped off in deep water. I was drowning, I went down the third time and Bill saw me and saved me. Thank you Lord, and thank you Bill. After that I learned how to swim. Sara told me that He saved several more in that pond.

When I was 12 years old, I went forward in church to be saved but was an act more or less because I saw other kids doing it. I knew of God and believed there was a God but didn't have Him in my heart. The Bible says that satan knows there is a God. I don't know my exact my age, maybe about 13 or 14. I started having some kind of seizures. They took me to the Doctor and in the Hospital, did all kinds of test and brain scans and never found the cause. The seizures got worse the older I got. I went thru my whole life with them, worked in high and dangerous places and would have one, but **God's hand was on me**. The other story is that I still have them. Ahh! I knew I skipped something. When I was 6 years old, I had appendicitis, had an operation and almost bled to death. I was bleeding from inside, Daddy came in hospital room and the bed was covered with blood. That's the **4th time God's hand on me**. When I was a little older they thought I had polio, a crippling disease. They had to draw fluid from my spine to test, it was not polio.

The **5th time God's hand was on me** was when I was 14. I had 2 best friends, their names were Bill Royal and Ronnie Bennett no kin. They both were in a bad car wreck. Jerry Wright was driving and lost control, went down a steep bank, flipped over and Ronnie got killed. His head was crushed in. Well, a few years later, Bill went to the army. He got killed in Vietnam. I just heard 2 weeks ago that he was recognized 50 years later to have saved someone when he got killed. They wouldn't take me cause of seizures. I couldn't understand why out of the 3 of us boys, I was still here. God had his plan and reason for this. I just didn't know what it was until later.

Joe C. Bennett
April 11, 2018

Chapter 20

MAKING MONEY BUT LOSING TIME

It was quiet; almost too quiet for a restaurant. I looked around and saw just the two young people who were there when I'd first come in. I was about say, "I guess it is time to go now," but Ruth quickly asked her last question: "What are you going to do now that you are retired?"

"I want to serve God full time," I answered. "That's my heart's desire. Joe must have known what I would be doing after he died, or perhaps he was just prophesying what would happen to me after he died because he made a comment that I should have married a pastor and then asked me if he had been a hindrance to the things that I wanted to do for God. I had to assure him that he was never a hindrance and that while there were times that he doubted my faith, he jumped right back in the wagon as soon as he knew where I was going. It was during this conversation that I told him that after he died, I planned to serve God full-time. He gave me his blessing by saying, 'May you have all the resources that you need.' That was my blessing, my gift from my husband.

"After he died, I had to go back to teaching as soon as I could because I was paying nearly $1000 dollars a month for health insurance. However, I didn't realize how much I had changed. While I was taking care of my husband, my daily prayer was: 'God, give patience!' But when I returned to teaching, I found that my patience had increased so much I'd lost my ability to teach in a prison.

"I'd lost the strictness I'd learned from Julia, which I relied on to maintain control of my students. Before I left, I'd had a reputation for being a 'good, but mean' teacher. When I returned, I was just a good teacher. I became a baby sitter to them. I clung to the notion that one day I'd get it all back and things would get better, but my guilt over not functioning the way I used to made me feel like I didn't belong there anymore.

"One day, while I was arranging books in my closet, it dawned on me – or perhaps God revealed to me – that I was making money, but I was losing time. Back when I was taking care of my husband, I'd been preparing myself to become a Bible teacher. So when the thought of making money but losing time came to me, I knew it was the time to suggest I take an early retirement. I needed to let them find a replacement for me since I was no longer an effective teacher there.

"The same day I filed for retirement, I was in a car accident that made it impossible for me to go back to work. So even if I'd changed my mind about retiring, I couldn't go back because of my injuries. That closed door affirmed that I'd made the right decision. Going back was no longer an option.

"When my former elementary co-teacher, Marybeth Pennington, asked me what I was going to do, I told her I would like to be a missionary. When she asked where I was going, I told her I was still praying about it. Remembering my excitement about learning Spanish, she suggested I consider Spanish-speaking countries. Not only that, she arranged for me to meet her parents, who were former missionary in Spain. Before I knew it, I was scheduled to go to Spain as a missionary!

"Oh, so you are you going to Spain!" exclaimed Aunt Julia.

"Yes, Auntie. I will be staying there for six months." I responded.

It was past 9:00 pm when we left the restaurant. We'd been there for almost three hours. As we stood to leave, Ruth commented that my story would be a good one to write down.

When I arrived back home to Tennessee, two more people told me to write down my story. When I realized that I couldn't go to Spain because of Covid-19, it gave me the perfect opportunity to put it down on paper.

Chapter 21

Discovering My Platform

BEFORE I WAS SCHEDULED TO GO to Spain, I started praying for a platform. I'd prepared myself to teach the Bible full-time even while I was still teaching at the prison, but I didn't know exactly how or where I should be teaching. I'd had invitations, but I felt I needed more time to decide.

On January 14, 2020, I went to the Philippines to visit my family and friends for two weeks before going to Spain as a missionary. While I was there, I started to hear news about Covid-19 and I prayed I'd be able to get back before it got worse; otherwise, I wouldn't be able to go to Spain. I made it safely back to Tennessee, but a week before my trip to Spain, I realized that my body was exhausted and not yet ready to travel. At the same time, this new coronavirus was expanding it's grip on the world. I knew I had to cancel my mission trip.

Being locked down for me was not really a problem because I needed to rest. It also gave me time to write my story. Two weeks after being locked down I called my cousin Jane, who was supposed to be editing my story, to see how it was going and she responded, "I am sorry! We have been locked down for two weeks already. I don't know how to live this way! I've lost my bearings and I am not accomplishing anything!"

She sounded so stressed out; I could picture her just pacing back and forth not knowing what to do. So I told her to calm down and meditate on Psalm 91.

"Ok, I am doing it now!" she said. Then she put the phone down. I sent her a text telling her to focus on spiritual productivity.

Two days later, I received a call from her inviting me to a family Bible study she'd just started on Facebook Messenger. "Of course!" I said, and that was the beginning of my Bible study groups. It started with just one, and then my cousin Pranin in Australia joined and created two more groups. Then I created five more groups. After eight weeks, we had eight groups!

The 9:00 pm (Philippine time) group is where I teach ladies who would like to create their own cell phone Bible study groups and how to create Bible lesson outlines. They have now spread their wings. After a month of daily Bible study and prayer, they too created their own groups increasing the number from eight to 23 groups!

It is currently May of 2020 and I just created the 24th group. This one was birthed because my friend from Greece requested that I pray for her sister's salvation. This latest group has her sisters, a niece and some nephews, as well as some friends. We maximize the eight cell phones that we're allowed to use. I believe this will continue to grow even after Covid-19 has passed because I encourage everyone in my groups to share what they've learned from God's word by creating their own groups, doing the same things we're doing with their own members.

That very first group, which started with just two people (my cousin Jane and nephew KC), increased by Ishan, Aunt Merced, Ridge and Aunt Sattie, Hianne and me. And it is still growing! It quadrupled in number, forcing us to create another Facebook account to accommodate everyone in one session. KC and Jane also just recently created a group with people from Canada.

What has happened to me during Covid-19 reminds me of Joseph's response to his brothers: "You meant it evil against me, but God meant it for God" (Genesis 50:20). What Covid-19 meant for evil, God meant for good, for me. Covid-19 locked me down, but God gave me an opportunity to teach His word. Who would have known that social media would become my platform? Only God! I don't even have to travel anywhere to do it. I can just stay right here at home, teaching Bible studies to people anywhere I can reach through social media. What blessing! What a ministry!

CPSIA information can be obtained
at www.ICGtesting.com
Printed in the USA
LVHW050340061120
670868LV00001B/1

9 781632 217783